At Sylvan, we believe that a lifelong love of learning begins at an early age, and we are glad you have chosen our resources to help your child experience the joy of mathematics to build critical reasoning skills. We know that the time you spend with your children reinforcing the lessons learned in school will contribute to their love of learning.

Success in math requires more than just memorizing basic facts and algorithms; it also requires children to make sense of size, shape, and numbers as they appear in the world. Children who can connect their understanding of math to the world around them will be ready for the challenges of mathematics as they advance to topics that are more complex.

At Sylvan we use a research-based, step-by-step process in teaching math that includes thought-provoking math problems and activities. As students increase their success as problem solvers, they become more confident. With increasing confidence, students build even more success. Our Page Per Day books are designed to help you to help your child build the skills and confidence that will contribute to success in school.

Included with your purchase of this Page Per Day book is a coupon for a discount at a participating Sylvan Learning center. We hope you will use this coupon to further your child's academic journey. To learn more about Sylvan and our innovative in-center programs, call 1-800-EDUCATE or visit www.SylvanLearning.com.

We look forward to partnering with you to support the development of a confident, well-prepared, independent learner.

The Sylvan Team

Tips for Math Success

Relate math to your child's world. Show your child how math is a part of everyday life, in cooking, shopping, and eating out. Use shopping with coupons or measuring ingredients as impromptu math lessons.

Approach math in different ways. Help your child solve math problems with different approaches to help your child clarify the concepts taught at school.

Help your child visualize. Pictures of animals, sections of an orange, or coin collections can help your child understand and apply math concepts such as sorting by attributes.

Talk through a problem. Encourage your child to think aloud while working through a math problem. Sometimes talking out loud can help your child figure out how to approach a problem. Model this by talking out loud while you do simple math tasks, like doubling a recipe or determining how long it will take to run errands.

Be sure your child shows all work. It's important for a child to work through a problem on paper, showing each step. This can make it easier to go back if he or she needs to correct a mistake.

Offer homework support. If your child needs help, ask questions to guide your child toward the solution. Don't do the problem for your child. Ask about hints in the instructions or have your child explain the problem.

Determine mastery. Most math skills build on earlier skills. Be sure your child has mastered each milestone before moving on.

1st Grade Page Per Day:
Math Skills

Published in the United States by Random House, Inc., New York, and in Canada by
Random House of Canada Limited, Toronto.

www.tutoring.sylvanlearning.com

Producer & Editorial Direction: The Linguistic Edge
Writer: Amy Kraft
Cover and Interior Illustrations: Shawn Finley, Tim Goldman, and Duendes del Sur
Layout and Art Direction: SunDried Penguin

First Edition

ISBN: 978-0-307-94460-3
ISSN: 2161-9794

This book is available at special discounts for bulk purchases for sales promotions or premiums.
For more information, write to Special Markets/Premium Sales, 1745 Broadway, MD 6-2,
New York, New York 10019 or e-mail specialmarkets@randomhouse.com.

PRINTED IN THE USA

10 9 8 7 6 5 4

Practice the Numbers

COUNT the cubes. Then TRACE each number and word.

     1   one

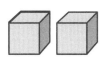   2   two

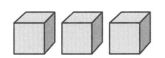   3   three

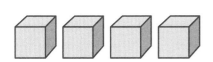   4   four

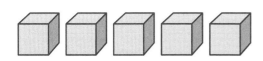   5   five

Counting to 10

Practice the Numbers

COUNT the cubes. Then TRACE each number and word.

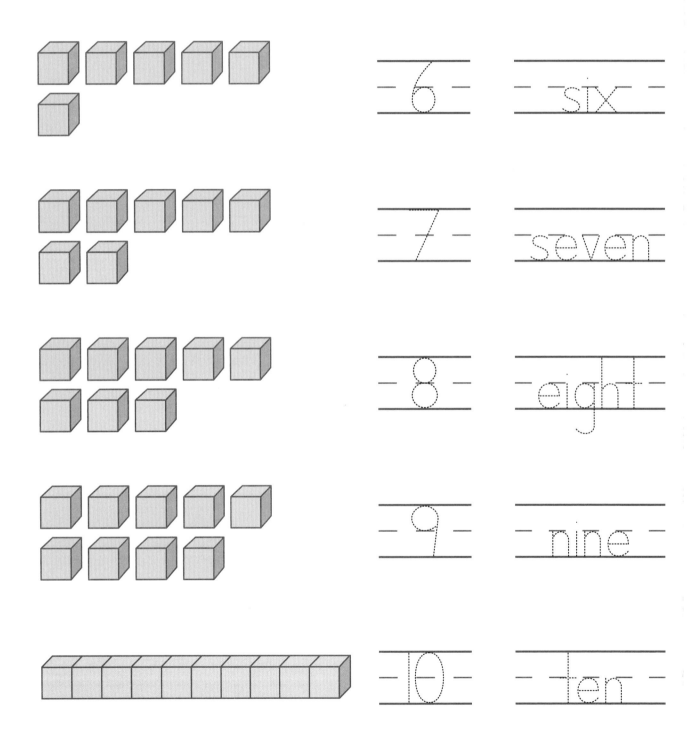

6   six

7   seven

8   eight

9   nine

10   ten

Color Groups

LOOK at each number. COLOR the correct number of jellybeans to match the number.

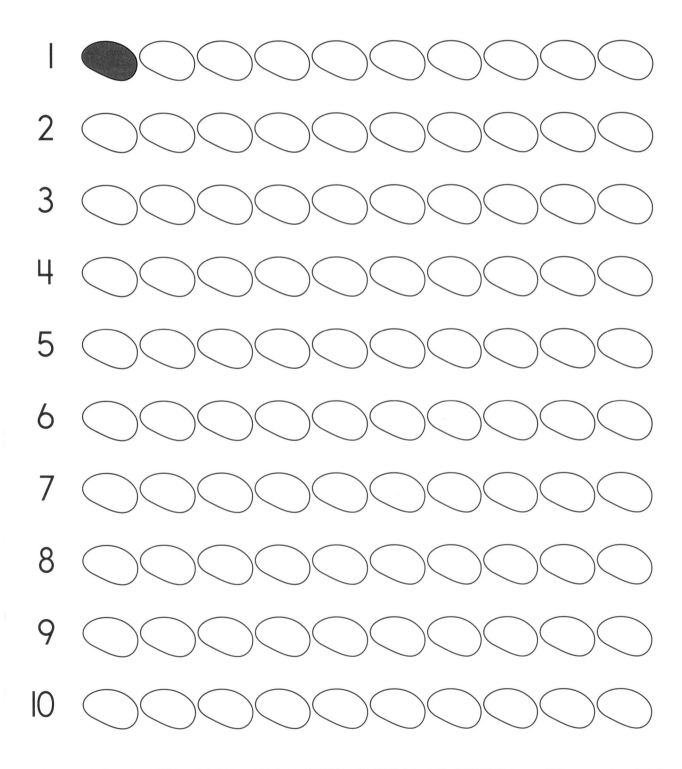

1

2

3

4

5

6

7

8

9

10

Match Up

DRAW lines to connect the numbers and pictures that go together.

7

10

9

6

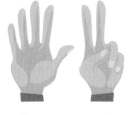

4

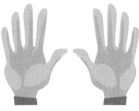

3

Picture It

WRITE the number of pieces of candy you see in each jar. ADD the two numbers, and WRITE how much candy there is in both jars.

1.

$$5 + 1 = 6$$

2.

$$\square + \square = \square$$

3.
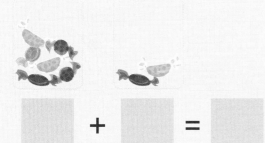

$$\square + \square = \square$$

4.
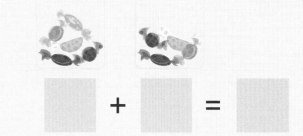

$$\square + \square = \square$$

5.

$$\square + \square = \square$$

6.
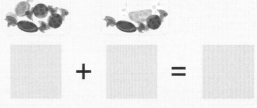

$$\square + \square = \square$$

Marble Mania

WRITE the number of marbles you see. ADD the two numbers, and WRITE the total number of marbles.

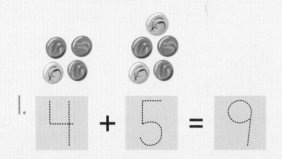

1. 4 + 5 = 9

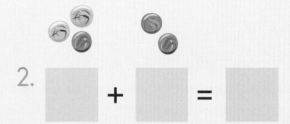

2. ☐ + ☐ = ☐

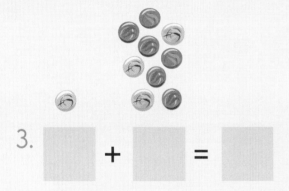

3. ☐ + ☐ = ☐

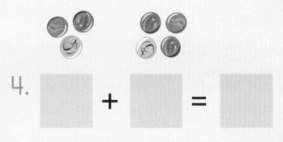

4. ☐ + ☐ = ☐

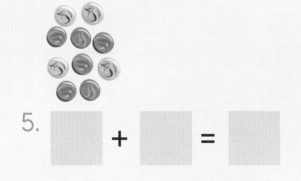

5. ☐ + ☐ = ☐

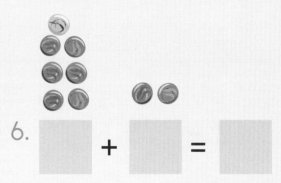

6. ☐ + ☐ = ☐

Bug Collection

WRITE the missing number. HINT: Count the bugs to help you.

1.

$$2 \; + \; \boxed{} \; = \; 5$$

2.

$$\boxed{} \; + \; 1 \; = \; 8$$

3.

$$\boxed{} \; + \; 4 \; = \; 9$$

4.

$$4 \; + \; \boxed{} \; = \; 10$$

5.

$$6 \; + \; \boxed{} \; = \; 7$$

6.

$$\boxed{} \; + \; 3 \; = \; 6$$

Adding Sums to 10

It All Adds Up

WRITE each sum.

1. 7
   + 2
   ⬜

2. 3
   + 5
   ⬜

3. 4
   + 1
   ⬜

4. 6
   + 2
   ⬜

5. 10
   + 0
   ⬜

6. 2
   + 1
   ⬜

7. 7
   + 3
   ⬜

8. 5
   + 4
   ⬜

9. 1
   + 9
   ⬜

10. 5
   + 2
   ⬜

11. 8
   + 1
   ⬜

12. 0
   + 7
   ⬜

13. 2
   + 2
   ⬜

14. 4
   + 3
   ⬜

15. 6
   + 1
   ⬜

16. 4
   + 4
   ⬜

The Cupcake Eater

How many cupcakes are left on the plate after the Cupcake Eater eats some? WRITE the answer.

HINT: Cross off the number of eaten cupcakes, and count how many are left.

1.  $4 - 1 =$ 3
    cupcakes   eaten

2.  $5 - 3 =$

3.  $7 - 2 =$

4.  $8 - 6 =$

Cracking Eggs

DRAW cracks on the eggs, and COUNT how many eggs are left. WRITE the number.

1. 5 eggs
   − 2 cracked eggs
   ___
   3

2. 8
   − 4
   ___

3. 7
   − 1
   ___

4. 9
   − 4
   ___

5. 3
   − 1
   ___

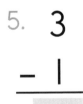

6. 10
   − 5
   ___

Bowled Over

Each row shows how many pins were standing at the start and end of a bowling turn. WRITE the number of pins that were knocked over.

1. $10 - \boxed{} = 5$

2. $10 - \boxed{} = 8$

3. $8 - \boxed{} = 4$

4. $4 - \boxed{} = 1$

5. $6 - \boxed{} = 2$

6. $7 - \boxed{} = 3$

Subtracting Differences from 10

What's the Difference?

WRITE each difference.

1. 8
   − 2

2. 9
   − 7

3. 4
   − 3

4. 5
   − 1

5. 10
   − 9

6. 6
   − 4

7. 1
   − 0

8. 7
   − 2

9. 3
   − 1

10. 5
    − 5

11. 9
    − 3

12. 10
    − 7

13. 4
    − 0

14. 9
    − 8

15. 3
    − 2

16. 8
    − 5

Practice the Numbers

COUNT the cubes. Then TRACE each number and word.

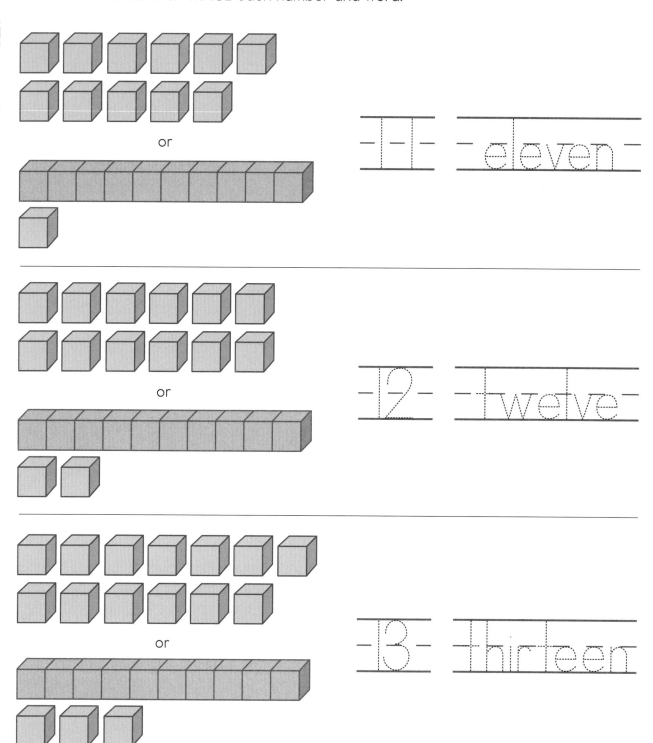

Counting to 20

Chart Smart

This chart shows how many people like different foods for lunch. COUNT how many people like each kind of food. Then WRITE the number.

Pizza	(pizza slices)
Sandwich	(sandwiches)
Chili	(chili bowls)
Hamburger	(hamburgers)

| 1 | 2 | 3 | 4 |

Practice the Numbers

COUNT the cubes. Then TRACE each number and word.

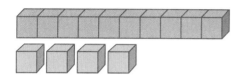 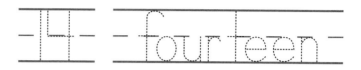

14 fourteen

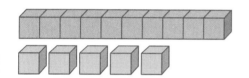 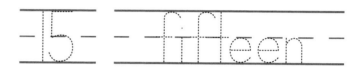

15 fifteen

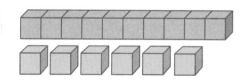 

16 sixteen

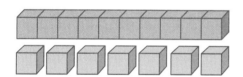

17 seventeen

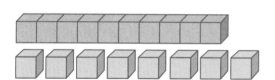

18 eighteen

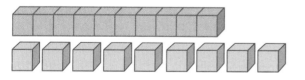

19 nineteen

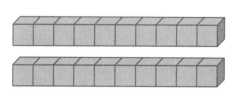

20 twenty

Loop It

LOOK at each number. CIRCLE the correct number of jellybeans to match the number.

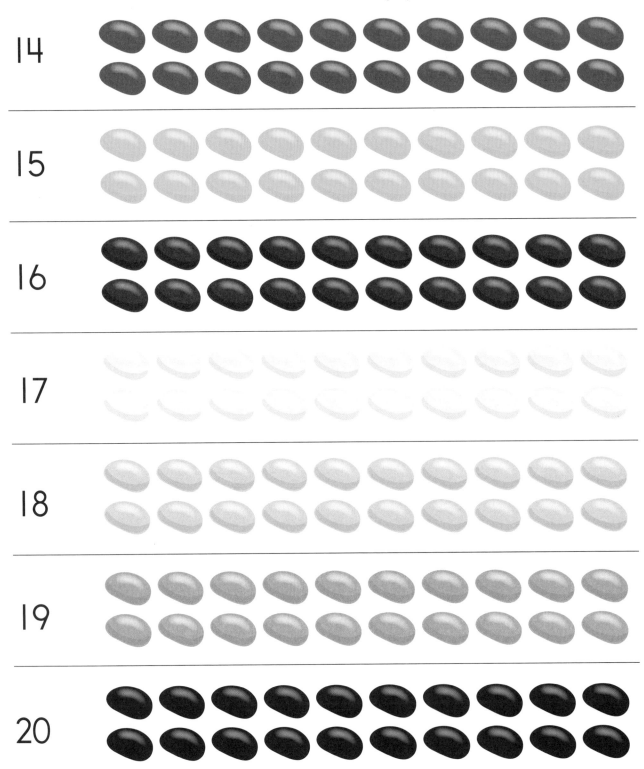

14

15

16

17

18

19

20

Picture It

WRITE each sum.

$$12$$
$$+\ 2$$

1

$$10$$
$$+\ 8$$

2

$$9$$
$$+\ 3$$

3

$$16$$
$$+\ 4$$

4

$$14$$
$$+\ 5$$

5

$$13$$
$$+\ 6$$

6

Chart Smart

This chart shows how many kids like to play diffe[...]nber of kids who like each sport. Then ADD the numbers.

2=3

Basketball	
Football	
Hockey	
Baseball	
Soccer	
Tennis	

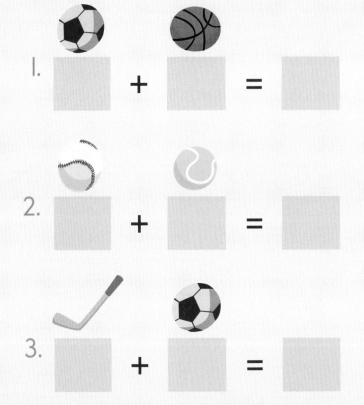

1. ☐ + ☐ = ☐

2. ☐ + ☐ = ☐

3. ☐ + ☐ = ☐

Rock-Star Kids

ADD the scores of each performer.
CIRCLE the performer with the most points.

8	7	3

8	5	7

6	6	4

5	8	6

It All Adds Up

WRITE each sum.

1. 10
   + 3
   ____

2. 14
   + 3
   ____

3. 9
   + 5
   ____

4. 17
   + 2
   ____

5. 13
   + 6
   ____

6. 20
   + 0
   ____

7. 8
   + 9
   ____

8. 7
   + 7
   ____

9. 11
   + 9
   ____

10. 16
   + 1
   ____

11. 7
   + 5
   ____

12. 12
   + 4
   ____

13. 15
   + 3
   ____

14. 11
   + 5
   ____

15. 13
   + 0
   ____

16. 8
   + 6
   ____

The Chocolate Eater

How many chocolates are left on the plate after the Chocolate Eater eats some? WRITE the answer.

HINT: Cross off the number of eaten chocolates, and count how many are left.

1.

$13 - 5 =$

2.

$17 - 4 =$

3.

$15 - 8 =$

4.

$20 - 9 =$

Subtracting Differences from 20

Cracking Eggs

DRAW cracks on the eggs, and COUNT how many eggs are left. WRITE the number.

1.   12
    − 7
    ⬚

2.   18
    − 4
    ⬚

3.   14
    − 7
    ⬚

4.   11
    − 6
    ⬚

5.   16
    − 10
    ⬚

6.   19
    − 9
    ⬚

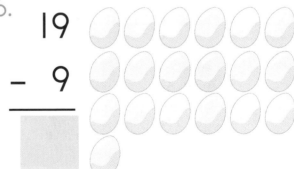

Balloon Pop

Each row shows how many balloons there were at the start of the party . . . and later after some popped. WRITE the number of balloons that popped.

1.

2.

3.

4.

5.

6.

Subtracting Differences from 20

What's the Difference?

WRITE each difference.

1. $\begin{array}{r} 11 \\ -\ 4 \\ \hline \end{array}$

2. $\begin{array}{r} 16 \\ -\ 7 \\ \hline \end{array}$

3. $\begin{array}{r} 20 \\ -11 \\ \hline \end{array}$

4. $\begin{array}{r} 18 \\ -\ 8 \\ \hline \end{array}$

5. $\begin{array}{r} 17 \\ -13 \\ \hline \end{array}$

6. $\begin{array}{r} 14 \\ -\ 0 \\ \hline \end{array}$

7. $\begin{array}{r} 19 \\ -\ 3 \\ \hline \end{array}$

8. $\begin{array}{r} 15 \\ -14 \\ \hline \end{array}$

9. $\begin{array}{r} 12 \\ -\ 8 \\ \hline \end{array}$

10. $\begin{array}{r} 20 \\ -\ 6 \\ \hline \end{array}$

11. $\begin{array}{r} 13 \\ -10 \\ \hline \end{array}$

12. $\begin{array}{r} 17 \\ -\ 5 \\ \hline \end{array}$

13. $\begin{array}{r} 18 \\ -16 \\ \hline \end{array}$

14. $\begin{array}{r} 11 \\ -\ 1 \\ \hline \end{array}$

15. $\begin{array}{r} 15 \\ -\ 5 \\ \hline \end{array}$

16. $\begin{array}{r} 14 \\ -\ 8 \\ \hline \end{array}$

Practice the Numbers

TRACE each number and word.

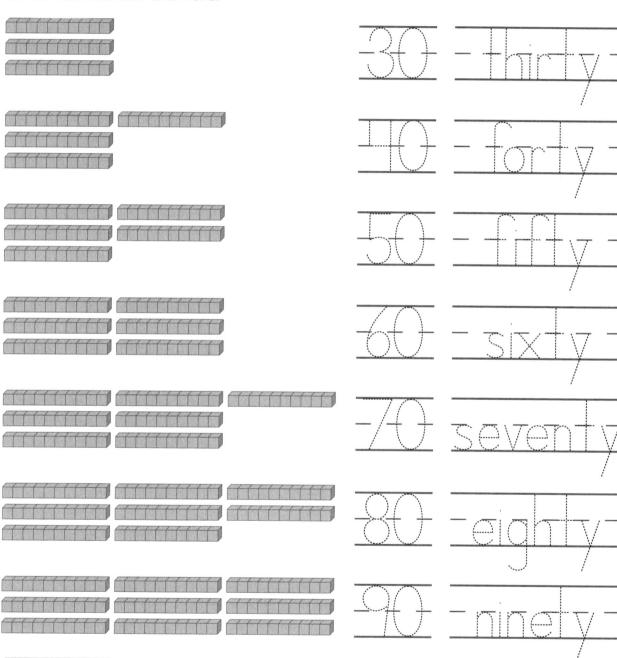

30 thirty

40 forty

50 fifty

60 sixty

70 seventy

80 eighty

90 ninety

100 one hundred

Match Up

DRAW lines to connect the numbers and pictures that go together.

80

30

50

90

60

100

40

70

Color Clash

COLOR the numbers in the chart using the colors shown.

41		33	
28		79	
67		84	
95		16	
50		72	

1	2	3	4	5	6	7	8	9	10
11	12	13	14	15	16	17	18	19	20
21	22	23	24	25	26	27	28	29	30
31	32	33	34	35	36	37	38	39	40
41	42	43	44	45	46	47	48	49	50
51	52	53	54	55	56	57	58	59	60
61	62	63	64	65	66	67	68	69	70
71	72	73	74	75	76	77	78	79	80
81	82	83	84	85	86	87	88	89	90
91	92	93	94	95	96	97	98	99	100

Bug Collection

CIRCLE groups of 10 to help you count. Then WRITE the number of bugs.

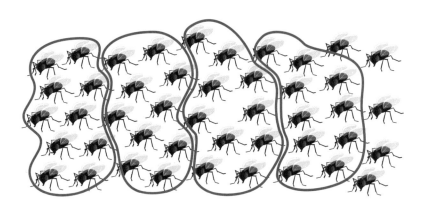

 flies

1

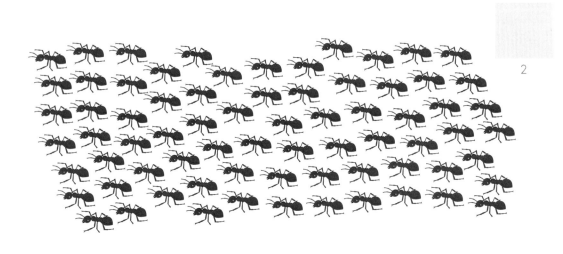

ants

2

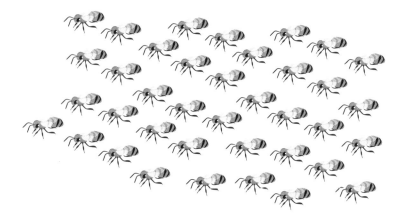

bees

3

Get in P

WRITE how ~~ ee. Then WRITE the number they make.

2-3

1.
	Ones
	3

/3

2.
Tens	Ones

3.
Tens	Ones

4.
Tens	Ones

5.
Tens	Ones

6.
Tens	Ones

7.
Tens	Ones

8.
Tens	Ones

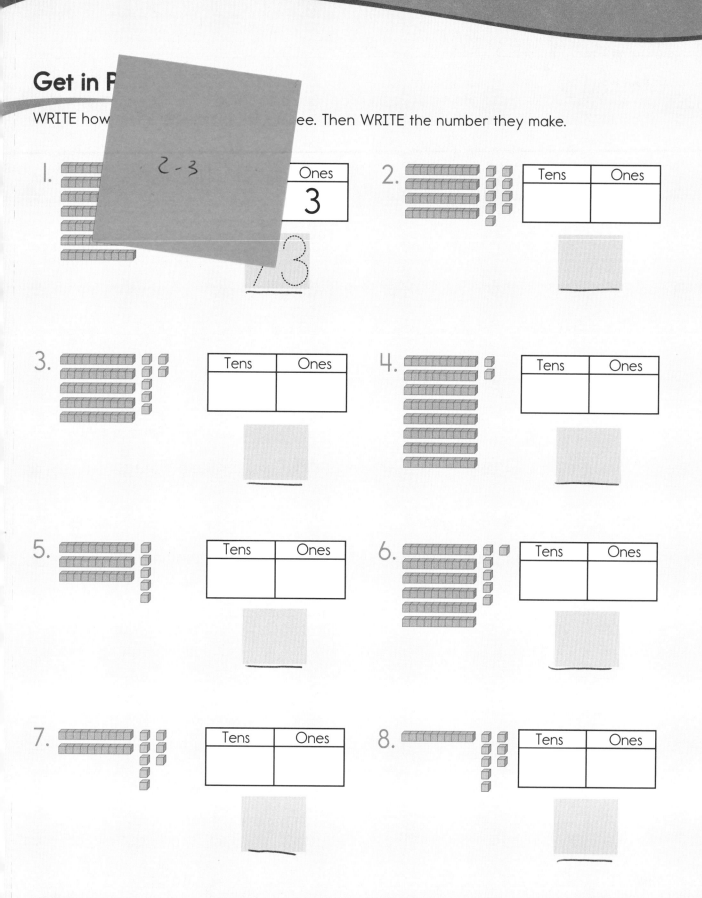

Match Up

DRAW lines to connect the numbers and pictures that go together.

87

29

41

77

65

36

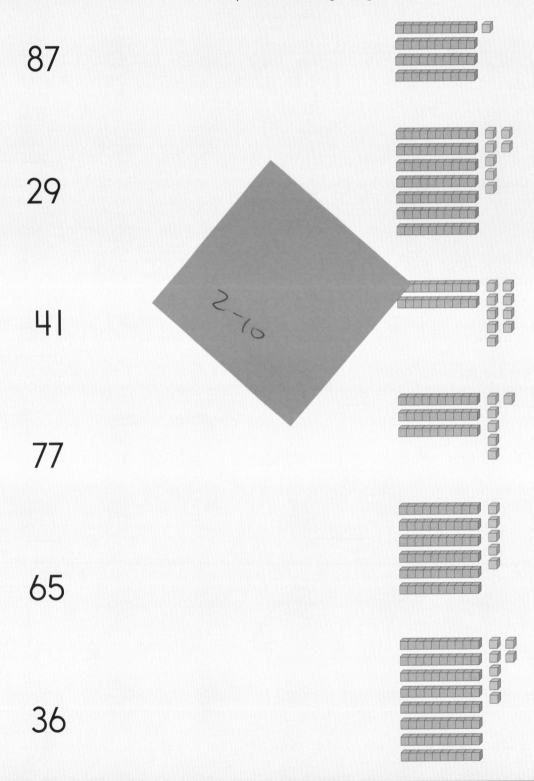

Compare

COUNT how many hundreds, tens, and ones you see. Then WRITE the number they make.

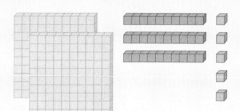

Hundreds	Tens	Ones

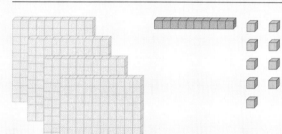

Hundreds	Tens	Ones

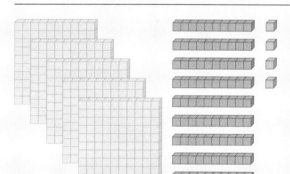

Hundreds	Tens	Ones

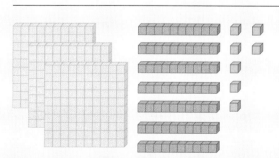

Hundreds	Tens	Ones

Number Match

CIRCLE the picture in each row that matches the number.

628
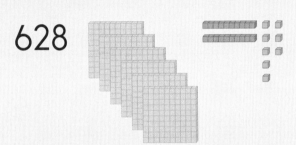 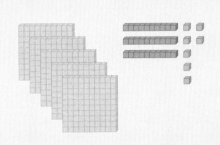

173
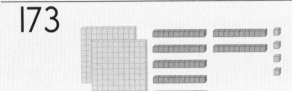 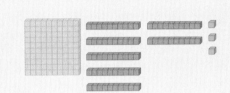

466
 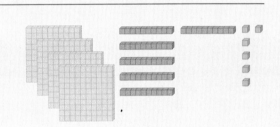

381
 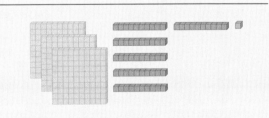

535
 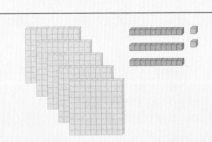

Get in Line

WRITE the missing numbers on each number line.

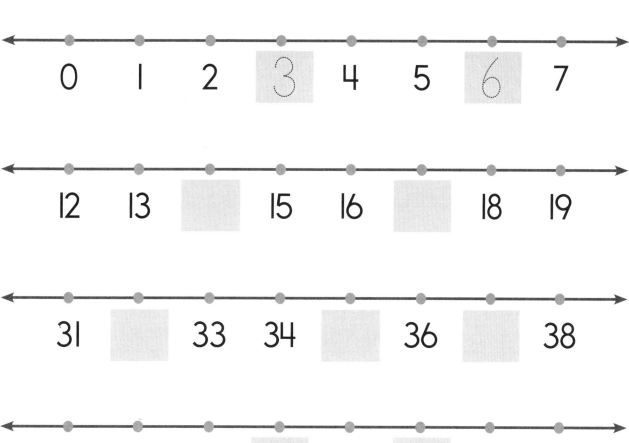

0   1   2   3   4   5   6   7

12   13   ▢   15   16   ▢   18   19

31   ▢   33   34   ▢   36   ▢   38

53   54   55   ▢   57   ▢   59   60

▢   66   67   ▢   69   70   ▢   72

76   ▢   78   79   80   ▢   82   83

Color Clash

Starting at number 2, sk ... the squares red.
Starting at number 5, sk ... the squares blue.

2-3

1	2	3			6	7	8	9	10
11	12	13	14	15	16	17	18	19	20
21	22	23	24	25	26	27	28	29	30
31	32	33	34	35	36	37	38	39	40
41	42	43	44	45	46	47	48	49	50
51	52	53	54	55	56	57	58	59	60
61	62	63	64	65	66	67	68	69	70
71	72	73	74	75	76	77	78	79	80
81	82	83	84	85	86	87	88	89	90
91	92	93	94	95	96	97	98	99	100

Which One?

CIRCLE the picture that has **more** than the other.

Which One?

CIRCLE the picture that has **less** than the other.

Find the Same

CIRCLE the shape in each row that is the same shape as the first shape.

Match Up

DRAW lines to connect the shapes that are the same.

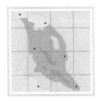

Find the Same

CIRCLE the shape in each row that is the same shape as the first shape.

1.

2.

3.

4.

5.

6.

Hide and Seek

LOOK at the shapes. DRAW a line to connect each shape with the object in the picture that has the same shape.

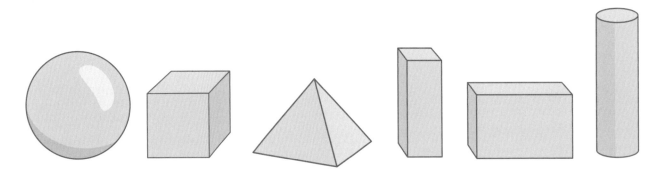

Match Up

DRAW lines to connect the layered shapes with the separated shapes.

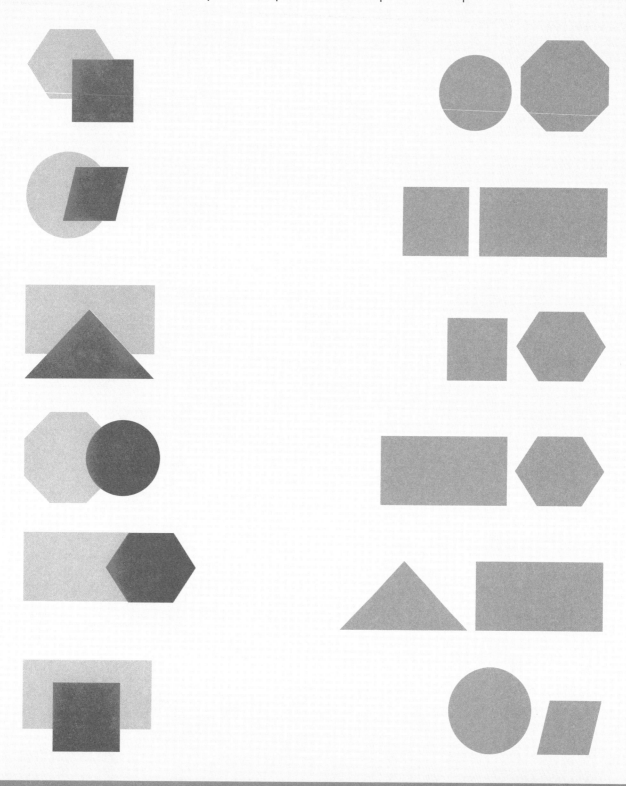

Match Up

DRAW a line to connect each shape that has been cut in half with its matching whole shape.

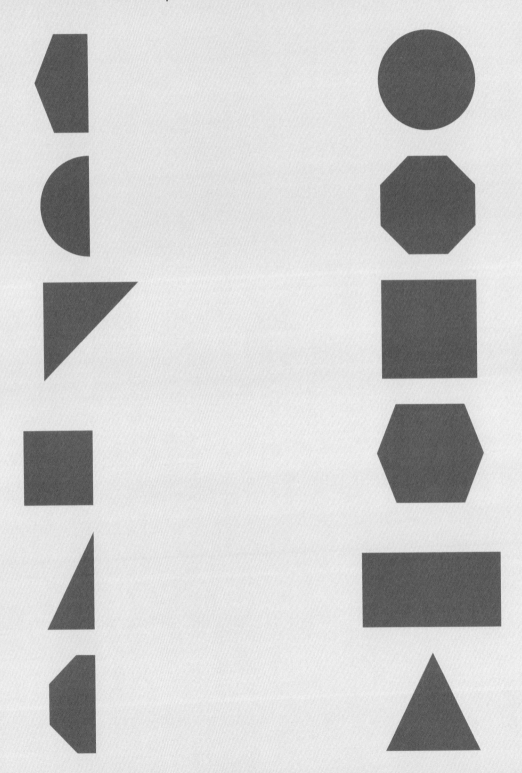

Mirror, Mirror

A shape has **symmetry** if a line can divide the shape so each half is a mirror image of the other. DRAW a line of symmetry through each picture.

Line of symmetry

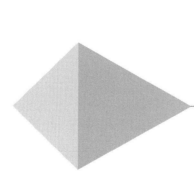

Shape Up

DRAW the mirror image of each shape, making it symmetrical.

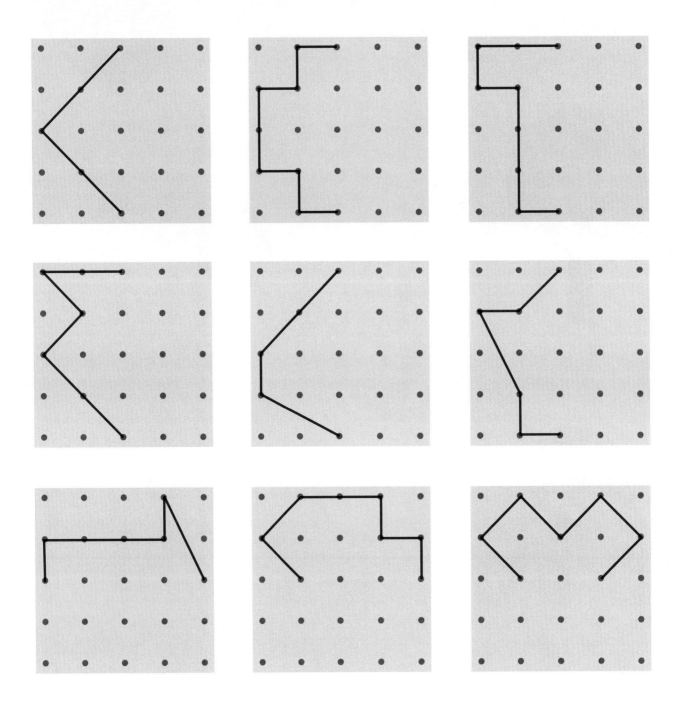

Measure Up

MEASURE the length of each object in

2–10

[ ] paper clips
1

[ ] paper clips
2

[ ] paper clips
3

[ ] paper clips
4

[ ] paper clips
5

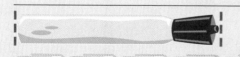

[ ] paper clips
6

[ ] paper clips
7

Measure Up

MEASURE the height of each object in people.

1
people

2
people

3
people

Watch It!

DRAW a line to connect each watch to a clock that shows the same time.

Give Me a Hand

DRAW the hour hand to match the time.

1. 11:00

2. 6:00

3. 3:00

4. 10:00

5. 7:00

6. 9:00

7. 4:00

8. 1:00

Watch It!

DRAW a line to connect each watch to a clock that shows the same time.

Telling Time in Half Hours

Give Me a Hand

DRAW the hour a... the time.

5:30

1-21-20

12:30

8:30

1:30

2:30

4:30

11:30

3:30

Which One?

CIRCLE the group of coins that matches each number.

1¢
penny

5¢
nickel

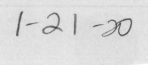

1-21-20

10¢
dime

25¢
quarter

5¢	13¢

7¢	14¢

23¢	31¢

Odd One Out

CROSS OUT the picture ~~that~~ ~~that~~ that does not match the others.

2-3

Match Up

DRAW lines to connect coins with the object that can be bought using exact change.

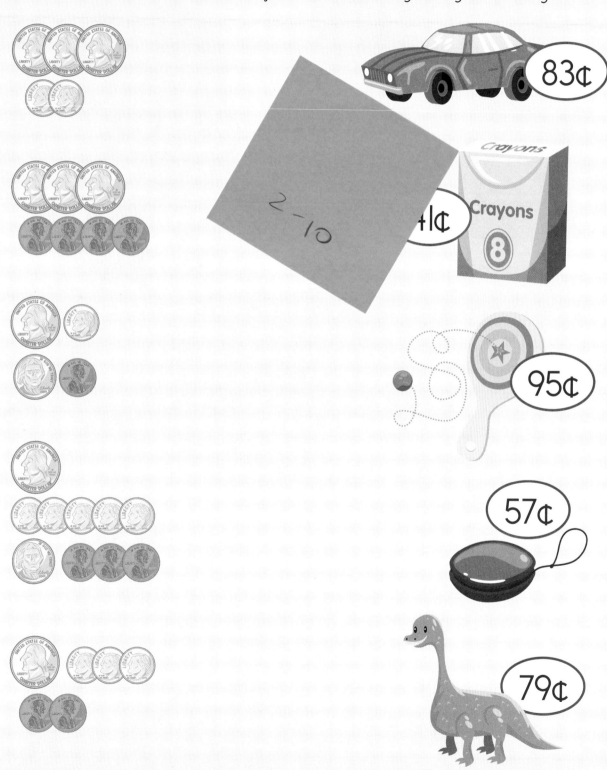

Using Coins

Can You Buy It?

COUNT the coins to see if there is enough money to buy each food. CIRCLE **yes** or **no**.

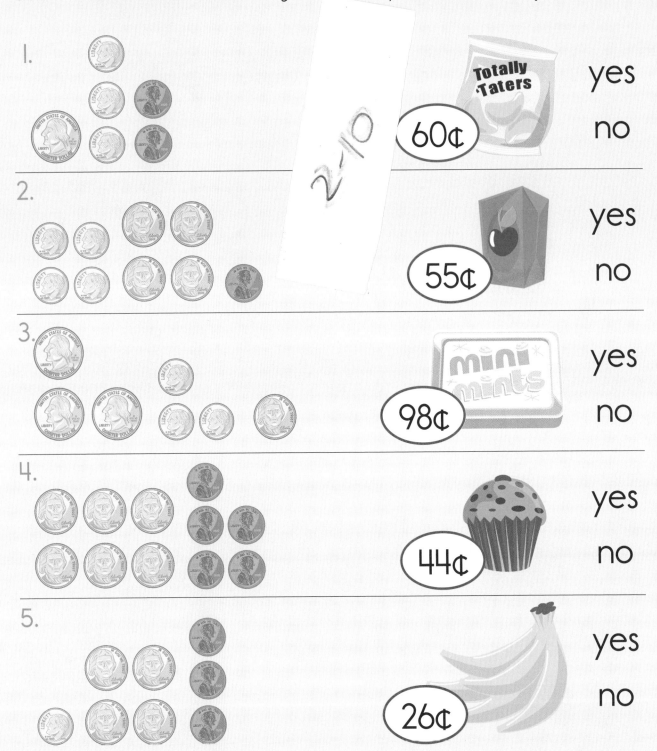

1. 60¢   yes   no

2. 55¢   yes   no

3. 98¢   yes   no

4. 44¢   yes   no

5. 26¢   yes   no

Answers

Page 5

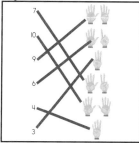

Page 6

Page 7
1. 5 + 1 = 6   2. 2 + 3 = 5
3. 6 + 2 = 8   4. 5 + 4 = 9
5. 3 + 7 = 10   6. 4 + 3 = 7

Page 8
1. 4 + 5 = 9
2. 3 + 2 = 5
3. 1 + 9 = 10
4. 3 + 4 = 7
5. 10 + 0 = 10
6. 7 + 2 = 9

Page 9
1. 3
2. 7
3. 5
4. 6
5. 1
6. 3

Page 10
1. 9   2. 8
3. 5   4. 8
5. 10   6. 3
7. 10   8. 9
9. 10   10. 7
11. 9   12. 7
13. 4   14. 7
15. 7   16. 8

Page 11
1. 3   2. 2
3. 5   4. 2

Page 12
1. 3   2. 4
3. 6   4. 5
5. 2   6. 5

Page 13
1. 5
2. 2
3. 4
4. 3
5. 4
6. 4

Page 14
1. 6   2. 2
3. 1   4. 4
5. 1   6. 2
7. 1   8. 5
9. 2   10. 0
11. 6   12. 3
13. 4   14. 1
15. 1   16. 3

Page 16
1. 13   2. 11
3. 12   4. 10

Page 18

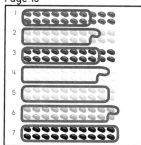

Page 19
1. 14   2. 18
3. 12   4. 20
5. 19   6. 19

Page 20
1. 5 + 8 = 13
2. 10 + 9 = 19
3. 12 + 5 = 17

Page 21

Page 22
1. 13   2. 17
3. 14   4. 19
5. 19   6. 20
7. 17   8. 14
9. 20   10. 17
11. 12   12. 16
13. 18   14. 16
15. 13   16. 14

Page 23
1. 8   2. 13
3. 7   4. 11

Page 24
1. 5   2. 14
3. 7   4. 5
5. 6   6. 10

Page 25
1. 6
2. 9
3. 11
4. 11
5. 0
6. 9

Page 26
1. 7   2. 9
3. 9   4. 10
5. 4   6. 14
7. 16   8. 1
9. 4   10. 14
11. 3   12. 12
13. 2   14. 10
15. 10   16. 6

Page 28

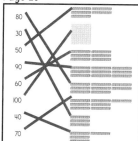

Page 29

1	2	3	4	5	6	7	8	9	10
11	12	13	14	15	16	17	18	19	20
21	22	23	24	25	26	27	28	29	30
31	32	33	34	35	36	37	38	39	40
41	42	43	44	45	46	47	48	49	50
51	52	53	54	55	56	57	58	59	60
61	62	63	64	65	66	67	68	69	70
71	72	73	74	75	76	77	78	79	80
81	82	83	84	85	86	87	88	89	90
91	92	93	94	95	96	97	98	99	100

Page 30
1. 45
2. 72
3. 38

Page 31
1. 7 tens, 3 ones, 73
2. 4 tens, 9 ones, 49
3. 5 tens, 7 ones, 57
4. 8 tens, 2 ones, 82
5. 3 tens, 5 ones, 35
6. 6 tens, 6 ones, 66
7. 2 tens, 8 ones, 28
8. 1 ten, 8 ones, 18

Answers

Page 32

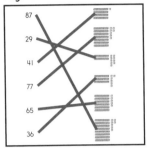

87
29
41
77
65
36

Page 33

1. 2 hundreds, 3 tens, 5 ones, 235
2. 4 hundreds, 1 ten, 9 ones, 419
3. 5 hundreds, 9 tens, 4 ones, 594
4. 3 hundreds, 7 tens, 7 ones, 377

Page 34

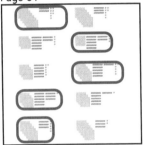

Page 35

0	1	2	3	4	5	6	7
12	13	14	15	16	17	18	19
31	32	33	34	35	36	37	38
53	54	55	56	57	58	59	60
65	66	67	68	69	70	71	72
76	77	78	79	80	81	82	83

Page 36

1	2	3	4	5	6	7	8	9	10
11	12	13	14	15	16	17	18	19	20
21	22	23	24	25	26	27	28	29	30
31	32	33	34	35	36	37	38	39	40
41	42	43	44	45	46	47	48	49	50
51	52	53	54	55	56	57	58	59	60
61	62	63	64	65	66	67	68	69	70
71	72	73	74	75	76	77	78	79	80
81	82	83	84	85	86	87	88	89	90
91	92	93	94	95	96	97	98	99	100

Page 37

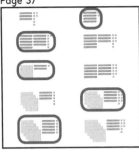

Page 38

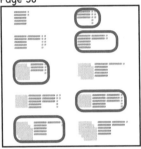

Page 39

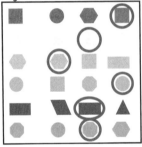

Page 40

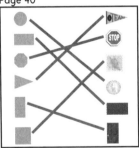

Page 41

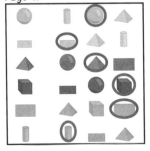

Page 42

Page 43

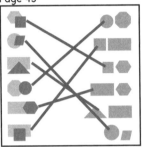

Page 44

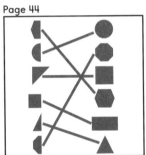

Page 45

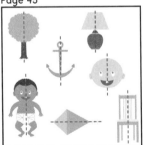

Page 46

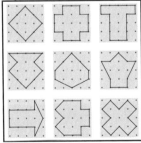

Page 47
1. 6
2. 4
3. 3
4. 6
5. 2
6. 4
7. 3

Page 48
1. 6
2. 13
3. 4

Page 49

Page 50

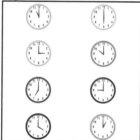

Page 51

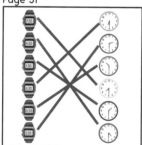

Page 52

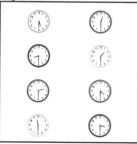

Page 53

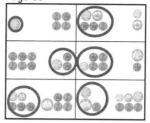

Page 54

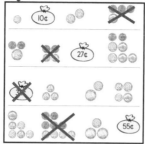

Page 55

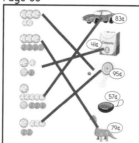

Page 56
1. no
2. yes
3. yes
4. no
5. yes

Check out Sylvan's complete line of offerings!

SINGLE-SUBJECT WORKBOOKS

- ✔ Pre-K–5th grade
- ✔ Focus on individual skills and subjects
- ✔ Fun activities and exercises

3-IN-1 SUPER WORKBOOKS

- ✔ Pre-K–5th grade
- ✔ Three Sylvan single-subject workbooks in one package
- ✔ Perfect practice for the student who needs to focus on a range of topics

A $39 value for just $18.99!

FUN ON THE RUN ACTIVITY BOOKS

- ✔ Kindergarten–2nd grade
- ✔ Just $3.99/$4.75 Can.
- ✔ Colorful games and activities for on-the-go learning

FLASHCARD SETS

- ✔ Spelling for Kindergarten–2nd grade
- ✔ Vocabulary for 3rd–5th grade
- ✔ Includes 230 words to help students reinforce skills

PAGE PER DAY WORKBOOKS

- ✔ Pre-K–1st grade
- ✔ Perforated pages—perfect for your child to do just one workbook page each day
- ✔ Extra practice the easy way!

Try FREE pages today at SylvanPagePerDay.com

With just a **PAGE PER DAY**, your child gets extra practice ... the easy way! Get sample pages for free!

Whether the goal is to get a jumpstart on new material or to brush up on past lessons, setting aside a small amount of time each day to complete one Sylvan workbook page will help your child review and improve skills, grow self-confidence, and develop a love of learning.

Visit **SylvanPagePerDay.com** to get free workbook printables in the grade of your choice!

Sylvan
Learning